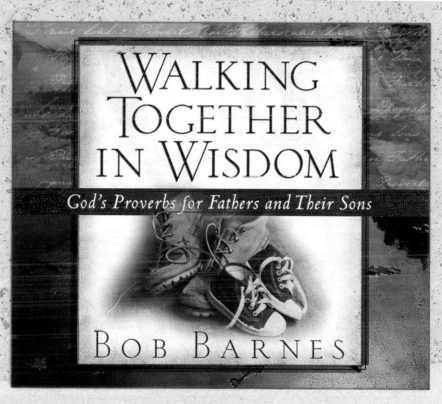

# WALKING TOGETHER IN WISDOM

*God's Proverbs for Fathers and Their Sons*

## BOB BARNES

HARVEST HOUSE PUBLISHERS
Eugene, Oregon

**Walking Together in Wisdom**

Text Copyright © 2001 by Harvest House Publishers

Eugene, Oregon 97402

Library of Congress Cataloging-in-Publication Data

Barnes, Bob, 1933-
    Walking together in wisdom / Bob Barnes.
        p. cm.
    ISBN: 0-7369-0434-4
    1. Bible. O.T. Proverbs—Criticism, interpretation, etc. 2. Fathers—Religious life.
I. Title.

    BS1465.2 .B33 2001
    223'706—dc21

                                                                    00-059753

Design and production by Garborg Design Works, Minneapolis, Minnesota

Harvest House Publishers has made every effort to trace the ownership of all poems and quotes. In the event of a question arising from the use of a poem or quote, we regret any error made and will be pleased to make the necessary correction in future editions of this book.

Scripture quotations are taken from the New American Standard Bible®, ©1960, 1962, 1971, 1972, 1973, 1975, 1977 by The Lockman Foundation. Used by permission.

**Printed in Hong Kong.**

00 01 02 03 04 05 06 07 08 09  / NG /  10 9 8 7 6 5 4 3 2 1

# INTRODUCTION

When my son, Bradley, was 16 years old, we spent several months going through the 31 chapters of Proverbs. The words of wisdom that came through this book were so valuable to our relationship. We were able to discuss in great detail what it means to be a wise man and a man of God. We explored instructions for living, teachings on folly, sin, goodness, wealth, poverty, the tongue, pride, humility, justice, vengeance, strife, gluttony, love, lust, laziness, friends, the family, life, and death. Almost every facet of human relationships was covered, and we found the words of Proverbs to be applicable to all men everywhere.

Our study together was a very rewarding experience—and there's a reason for that. After all, the Book of Proverbs was intended as a primer about life and living it the sensible way. That makes it a perfect guide for young men today, who sometimes feel tossed back and forth by the winds of change, trying to decide what to believe and how to develop into the men that God wants them to become. What better model could a man have than the wisdom portrayed in this collection of writings through proverbs and songs?

Tradition has always held that King Solomon did write most of the sayings in this book, though some may have been written by others of his day. These proverbs were not so much popular sayings, though, as they are a distillation of wisdom from those who knew the law of God.

It is my desire that you will be so touched by the simple insights on each page of this book that you will want to study the complete writings in this wisdom-filled book.

May you find your own wisdom increasing as you read through these selected readings and—I hope—share them with a growing son.

*Bob Barnes*

# Dedication

This book is dedicated to all the fathers of this country who have the privilege of leaving a Christian legacy for their children. When life is over, may we stand before the throne of God and hear from our Lord, "Well done, good and faithful servant."

Former First Lady Barbara Bush once said that "the success of our country will not be determined by who is in the White House as much as who is in your house." May you be encouraged to be a father who leads, who wants to be the "take charge" guy in your home and to set the spiritual thermostat with your family.

No more fitting dedication could be given than to men who want to teach by word and example. You are truly a blessing to all who know you.

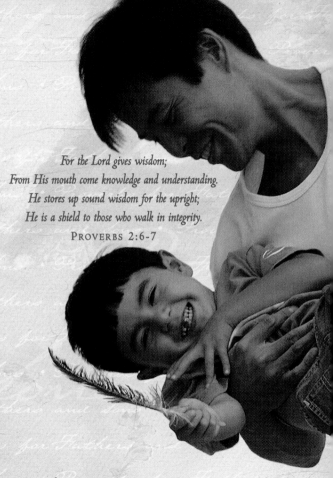

IF YOU GO TO GOD looking for knowledge and wisdom—you'll find it, and the wisdom that comes from God is the kind that will protect you. God is the giver of all good things. It just makes sense to listen as he speaks!

*For the Lord gives wisdom;*
*From His mouth come knowledge and understanding.*
*He stores up sound wisdom for the upright;*
*He is a shield to those who walk in integrity.*

PROVERBS 2:6-7

A LOT OF PEOPLE have the idea that following God is a big burden. But that's not the way it works in real life. Actually, when you open your heart to receive wisdom from God, you'll find that it's a pleasing thing. It actually feels good to be guided by God and follow his paths.

*For wisdom will enter your heart,*
*And knowledge will be pleasant to your soul.*

PROVERBS 2:10

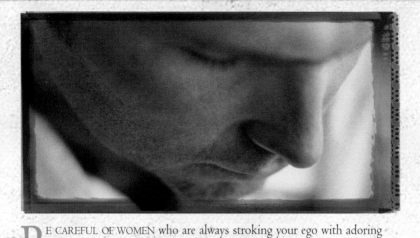

BE CAREFUL OF WOMEN who are always stroking your ego with adoring words. A woman like that can manipulate a man, betray him, and tempt him into doing things he knows are wrong. So watch out—and pray you'll be delivered from that kind of adulteress.

*Understanding will watch over you...*
*To deliver you from the strange woman,*
*From the adulteress who flatters with her words.*

PROVERBS 2:16

*Character is what you are in the dark.*
DWIGHT L. MOODY

IF YOU WANT TO BE God's kind of man, you'll strive to be both a loving man and an honest one! How do you do it? By pondering what these qualities mean—and by finding ways to weave them into your daily life. Practice looking out for others. Practice opening your mind to God's truth and your mouth to speak it. With every loving action and every honest word, you'll make love and truthfulness a part of your character.

*Do not let kindness and truth leave you;*
*Bind them around your neck,*
*Write them on the tablet of your heart.*
PROVERBS 3:3

Wʜᴀᴛ's ᴛʜᴇ sᴇᴄʀᴇᴛ of the truly wise man? He knows how to trust in the Lord—to seek God's wisdom, to listen for God's commands and obey them, and then to relax and let God take care of things. If you can do that, God will reward you with a blessing of a straight path. Your life will be a lot simpler and less confusing, with a lot fewer detours and ups and downs.

*Trust in the Lord with all your heart,*
*And do not lean on your own understanding.*
*In all your ways acknowledge Him,*
*And He will make your paths straight.*

Pʀᴏᴠᴇʀʙs 3:5-6

*Honor the Lord from your wealth,*
*And from the first of all your produce;*
*So your barns will be filled with plenty,*
*And your vats will overflow with new wine.*

PROVERBS 3:9-10

WHEN IT COMES to the good things life has to offer—both material possessions and spiritual blessings—a few important principles apply. First of all, it all comes from God—and ultimately it all belongs to him. Second, you'll have a lot more of it if you allow it to flow freely through your life. That means not hoarding the blessings for yourself, but passing them along in the form of tithes and offerings. When you do that, you're not really giving back to God—it's all his, remember! But you are getting yourself involved in God's work of making good things happen in the world—and that's a great honor.

THE WISE MAN will always have a good night's sleep because he has a pure heart! No more tossing and turning from unhealthy thoughts and guilty memories. No more wrestling with your conscience or worrying about what might happen tomorrow. No need to take a sleeping pill when you've chosen the way of wisdom.

*When you lie down, you will not be afraid;*
*When you lie down, your sleep will be sweet.*
PROVERBS 3:24

12

WHAT IS THE BEST WAY to understand who you are and where you have come from? Listen to your dad! His stories and even his lectures can tell you a lot about your family heritage, about what your dad believes is important, and about yourself, too. Even if your relationship is less that perfect, you can learn a lot from what your father has to say— and listening can make your relationship better. (By the way, this applies to your mom, too.)

*Hear, O sons, the instruction of a father,*
*And give attention that you may gain understanding.*
PROVERBS 4:1

DID YOU KNOW that the light of righteousness can actually guide you through life? The more you experience doing what is right, the clearer your decisions of right and wrong will become. It starts out with the glimmer of the faint light of daybreak—you get a little sense of what is right and you act on it. As you continue to make right decisions (using the words of Scripture and dependable counselors to help you), everything becomes a lot clearer and brighter and less confusing. What once seemed murky and hard to distinguish takes on the intensity of the noonday sun. So don't worry if you sometimes seem to be walking along dimly lit paths. Keep on doing what you know to be right, and everything will get a lot clearer. There's no reason to stumble when wisdom provides the light.

*But the path of the righteous is like the light of the dawn, That shines brighter and brighter until the full day.*

PROVERBS 4:18

KNOW-IT-ALLS are almost always fools! A wise man is well aware how much he has to learn—and is willing to humble himself enough to learn it. You'll grow if you keep a healthy respect for what you just don't know. Keep your heart open to God's lessons and seek to grow through the instruction of wise men. Do you know any?

*The fear of the Lord is the beginning of knowledge;*
*Fools despise wisdom and instruction.*

PROVERBS 1:7

*Hear my son, your father's instruction,*
*And do not forsake your mother's teaching...*
PROVERBS 1:8

THE FAMILY IS A CRUCIAL UNIT of growth, instruction, and discipline—a warm, secure incubator for producing wise adults. And yes, some parents do a better job than others at this important task. But you can always learn something from your parents if you listen to them and honor them with your obedience. More important, when you listen and obey, you'll be practicing the very wisdom you want to have as an adult. Then, when you become a parent, you can live out that wisdom as you raise your own children in a warm, secure, home.

SOMETIMES THE BEST APPROACH to a situation really is to "just say no"! But saying no takes courage. This world offers so many enticements, so many opportunities for foolishness, cruelty, and weakness...so many chances to choose death instead of life. So be brave—and be ready to give a firm "No" to those who want to lead you astray. Shout it if you need to— "Satan, get behind me!"

*My son, if sinners entice you,*
*Do not consent.*
PROVERBS 1:10

*Let your fountain be blessed,*
*And rejoice in the wife of your youth.*
PROVERBS 5:18

Despite what the world (and sometimes your body) seems to tell you, you really will be happier in life if you seek your sexual satisfaction in your marriage. Promiscuity is such a waste—it brings nothing but hurt, guilt, and eventual emptiness. Why not invest your energies in showing love to the woman that God gives you? Then you'll live in a home that flows freely with the blessings of love!

I F YOU THINK IT'S REALLY possible to lead a secret life or keep a little pocket of sins concealed, you're just fooling yourself! Even if you manage to keep your deeds concealed from your neighbors (and the credit companies), you'll still be observed by God. Yes, God, like your mother, has eyes in the back of his head. So you'll live much more peacefully and comfortably if you live transparently, not doing anything you wouldn't want God to see.

*For the ways of a man are before the eyes of the Lord,*
*And He watches all his paths.*
PROVERBS 5:21

D O YOUR BEST to avoid liability for the debts of others. Don't cosign loans unless you are really willing to take on the debt cheerfully. Don't lend money to a friend, a relative, or a neighbor unless you are willing to *give* that amount to him or her. The key to financial success and peace of mind is to work diligently at your own affairs, deal honestly in your business dealings, and use your income to God's glory. But don't let yourself get caught in financial traps that breed resentment and anger—not to mention monetary disaster.

*My son, if you have become surety for your neighbor,*
*Have given a pledge for a stranger....*
*Deliver yourself like a gazelle from the hunter's hand.*
PROVERBS 6:1-5

HOW DO YOU PLEASE GOD? This verse paints a vivid picture of what *not* to do. Turn it around and you've got a helpful guideline for how to live: Cultivate a humble attitude and an honest heart. Refuse to take advantage of the weak or connive to get your own way. Resist temptation—even if that means running hard in the other direction. Avoid gossip and rumors, and do whatever you can to promote peace.

You'll have to have God's help to manage it all, of course—but that's how he works. You can always count on God to help you do what pleases him.

*There are six things which the Lord hates,*
*Yes, seven which are an abomination to Him:*
*Haughty eyes, a lying tongue,*
*And hands that shed innocent blood,*
*A heart that devises wicked plans,*
*Feet that run rapidly to evil,*
*A false witness who utters lies,*
*And one who spreads strife among brothers.*

PROVERBS 6:16-19

IF YOU PLAY WITH FIRE, you're going to get burned—and that's especially true when it comes to the burning of lust. Don't imagine you're strong enough to be an exception. It's much wiser—and less arrogant—to avoid situations where you might be tempted. There are places you are better off not visiting. There are people you shouldn't be alone with. There are circumstances you need to avoid. In your heart, you know what they are. If you're wise, you'll pay attention!

*Can a man take fire in his bosom,*
*and his clothes not be burned?*
*Or can a man walk on hot coals,*
*and his feet not be scorched?*
PROVERBS 6:27-28

IT'S AMAZING HOW EASILY a smart man can become a fool when a beautiful woman is involved! Good looks, sweet talk, flattery, and sexual enticement are hard for any man to resist—and how can you practice good judgment when you're being swayed by your own surging hormones and your puffed-up ego? The thing to do when you find yourself in such a tempting situation is to run—fast. Mumble whatever excuse you can think of and leave the room as quickly as possible. It might not feel like a smooth move—but it could save your soul, your sanity, and maybe even your life.

*With her many persuasions she entices him;*
*With her flattering lips she seduces him.*
*Suddenly he follows her,*
*As an ox goes to the slaughter.*
PROVERBS 7:21-22

DON'T BE FOOLED by the idea of "innocent" sexual pleasures. The simple truth is that sex has consequences—and sex outside of God's plan has painful consequences. Some are obvious—like accidental pregnancy and disease. Others are more subtle and hard to recognize—emotional letdowns, spiritual alienation, difficulties in later relationships. The momentary pleasures are just not worth the long-term or even eternal consequences. Trust the One who invented sex in the first place—it's better when you do it his way!

*Do not let your heart turn aside to her [adulterous] ways,*
*Do not stray into her paths,*
*For many are the victims she has cast down,*
*And numerous are all her slain.*
PROVERBS 7:25

24

*For he who finds me [wisdom] finds life,*
*And obtains favor from the Lord.*

PROVERBS 8:35

WHAT DO YOU THINK is the best thing that could happen to you in life? Winning the lottery would be nice. Becoming a millionaire could be useful. Finding the perfect person to share life with would be fantastic. But the truly best thing that can happen to us in life is to find wisdom—for along with wisdom we'll find life. That's the winning combination, the great warranty that comes with being human on earth. Even better, if we find wisdom, we will find favor with God. And that's the Grand Prize—better than all the others.

*A wise son makes a father glad,*
*But a foolish son is a grief to his mother.*

PROVERBS 10:1

YOUR WISE CHOICES and your foolish ones reflect not only on you, but also on those who love you—especially your father and your mother. You have the power to bring them joy or unhappiness simply by the kind of person you become. And you have the privilege of so honoring them—not out of guilt or obligation, but out of love. Make your parents proud, and you'll be happier, too.

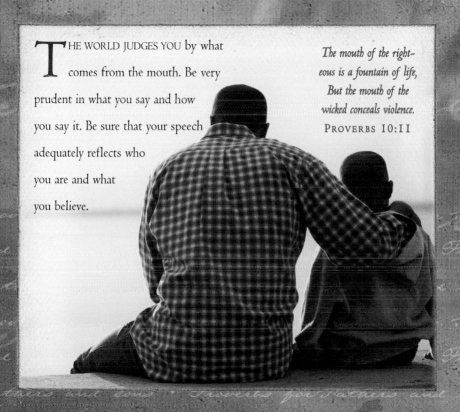

THE WORLD JUDGES YOU by what comes from the mouth. Be very prudent in what you say and how you say it. Be sure that your speech adequately reflects who you are and what you believe.

*The mouth of the righteous is a fountain of life, But the mouth of the wicked conceals violence.*

PROVERBS 10:11

WHEN WE SPEAK TOO LONG or too loudly, enjoying the sound of our own voice—that's when we're apt to say the wrong thing. The fact that God gave us all two ears and one mouth indicates that we are to listen twice as much as we are to speak. Sometimes it's really hard to hold our tongues—but we'll rarely have to apologize for words not spoken.

In fact, the only words we should apologize for not saying are words of affection to those we love!

*When there are many words, transgression is unavoidable,*
*But he who restrains his lips is wise.*
PROVERBS 10:19

*What the wicked fears will come upon him,*
*And the desire of the righteous will be granted.*

PROVERBS 10:24

BE CAREFUL WHAT ATTITUDES you hold in your heart, because they determine your expectations and perhaps your future! A treacherous person cannot trust anybody. A cheat fears being cheated. A mean-spirited human being expects nothing but meanness from those around him. It's hard to think the best of the future when all you know is the worst. But the opposite is true as well. If you desire nothing but righteousness, that desire will become a self-fulfilling prophecy. What you seek, you will find!

*The righteous will never be shaken,*
*But the wicked will not dwell in the land.*

PROVERBS 10:30

CELEBRATE THE STABILITY that comes with a healthy fear of the Lord! The very process of seeking to draw closer to him builds a firm emotional and spiritual foundation. The more you come to know the Father, the more at home you will be in his presence. What a contrast to the emptiness and hopelessness of those who turn away from God's laws and thus exile themselves from the land of the blessed.

HONESTY IN OUR BUSINESS DEALINGS—not cheating others, not cutting corners, keeping our word—will almost always win us the respect of our colleagues and a good reputation in the marketplace. But even if such integrity doesn't bring business rewards, it's still worthwhile, because that's the approach that pleases God.

*No honest man ever repented of his honesty.*
GERMAN PROVERB

*A false balance is an abomination to the Lord,*
*But a just weight is His delight.*
PROVERBS 11:1

SOMETIMES IT SEEMS as if the world rewards the wrong people! Public immorality, official corruption, random violence, and just plain bad manners almost seem the standard of success, and the sleaziest, most indecent people seem to be making money, gaining fame, and being elected to office!

But don't be fooled. In the end, your attempt to be a righteous man, to live out the life that God has designed, will be rewarded. By your very life, you'll add to the joy in your family, neighborhood, city, state and nation— not to mention the joy that fills the heavens. Joy is the standard of the heart when the King lives there. And heartfelt joy by far the most fulfilling reward that earth and heaven has to offer.

*When it goes well with the righteous, the city rejoices,*
*And when the wicked perish, there is glad shouting.*
PROVERBS 11:10

*The generous man will*
*be prosperous,*
*And he who waters will*
*himself be watered.*
PROVERBS 11:25

I T'S A PRINCIPLE that goes against our most basic human instincts—but it has proved true again and again: The Lord gives generously to those who give generously. If we close our fists on what we have, guarding it and keeping it all for ourselves, we'll be left with just that paltry amount—or less. But if we open our hands and give of what we have—material goods as well as our talents and energies—our hands will remain open to receive more and more and more and more. It really works. We are rich only in what we give away.

*No man is free who cannot
command himself.*
PYTHAGORAS

BEING CORRECTED and disciplined is hard on the pride, but good for growth. Don't be stubborn and resist being taught by word and deed. Don't waste your energy resisting those in authority over you. Instead, take your ego down a notch, control your rebellious spirit, and *learn*.

*Whoever loves discipline loves knowledge,
But he who hates reproof is stupid.*
PROVERBS 12:1

34

*Better is he who is lightly*
*esteemed and has a servant,*
*Than he who honors himself*
*and lacks bread.*

PROVERBS 12:9

A MAN OF HUMBLE CIRCUMSTANCES
who works for himself may well
be better off than one who plays the big
shot but doesn't attend to the business
of taking care of himself. A man's best
reward for his work is not what he gets
for it... but what he becomes by it.

DON'T UNDERESTIMATE your ability to influence others. When you keep your promises and honor your commitments, when you notice people's needs and take the trouble to help, when you respond to snubs and insults with kindness and patience…people *do* notice. Of course, the same is true when you let people down, unleash your temper often, and get your own at the expense of others. You may never know the impact your life has on a neighbor or coworker—simply through the way you live. Actions truly do speak more loudly than words.

*The righteous is a guide to his neighbor,*
*But the way of the wicked leads them astray.*
PROVERBS 12:26

*The soul of the sluggard craves and gets nothing,*
*But the soul of the diligent is made fat.*
### PROVERBS 13:4

LIFE ISN'T EASY for those who take it easy! That's because we all have a built-in, God-given need to work at our fullest capacities and achieve something meaningful and worthwhile. When we do that, we feel a sense of satisfaction. When we don't, we end up feeling empty and dissatisfied—even if we've lost the conscious desire to work.

It's possible, of course, to work very hard and still feel empty. That usually indicates either an attitude problem, an unsuitable occupation, or both. Almost any work can be meaningful when done "as to the Lord"—but the Lord can also help you find a job that challenges and satisfies you. Ask him to direct you—then start planning and preparing yourself.

W E NEED HOPE to live—but hope is not enough. It is only when we act on our hopes and our desires and step forward in faith that we discover the full, flowering riches the future has to offer us. It's not entirely up to us, of course. God is in charge of the future, and what he has in mind might be different from what we planned. But we still need to do *something* about our hopes—even if it's only bringing them to the Lord and trusting him to fulfill our future. Hope without some form of action on our part is not really hope at all—just an idle wish that can't come true.

Think of it this way. Plowing and planting seeds doesn't guarantee a harvest. But if we don't plow and plant—we guarantee there *won't* be a harvest.

*Hope deferred makes the heart sick,*
*But desire fulfilled is a tree of life.*
PROVERBS 13:12

38

*He who spares his rod hates his son,*
*But he who loves him disciplines him diligently.*

PROVERBS 13:24

"THIS HURTS ME more than it hurts you." You didn't believe it when your parents said it to you prior to discipline—but it's true. No loving parent relishes the prospect of making a child uncomfortable and unhappy. But a responsible parent knows that consequences applied now with love can prevent later, more painful consequences inflicted by life itself. If we love our children, we need to discipline them as God disciplines us—justly, lovingly, but also effectively. We need to be creative and imaginative in devising methods that fit the behavior and the individual. And we need always discipline prayerfully—depending on our heavenly Father to discipline us as well.

*Our lives will be complete only when we
express the full intent of the Master.*

CHARLES R. HEMBREE

*In the fear of the Lord there is strong confidence,
And his children will have refuge.*

PROVERBS 14:26

THE GREATEST GIFT you can give your children is to teach them—through both your words and your actions—to love God, to depend on him and respect his laws. If you do, they will have something real to base their lives on when they are grown and out of your care. They will have a firm foundation of faith on which to build secure, fulfilling lives.

ANGER, IN ITSELF, is just a normal human emotion. But hostility can also become a knee-jerk (and foolish) response to anything that thwarts our personal desires. It's a dangerous habit that wreaks havoc on our relationships and damages our health—but it can be broken. How? By learning alternate ways of responding to stress—such as meditation or exercise. By channeling the angry energy into positive activities—such as cleaning out the garage. By cultivating an understanding of why other people act the way they do—it's harder to erupt in anger when we can see the other person's point. But most of all, through developing the alternate habit of taking our frustrations immediately to God and relying on him to help us handle our anger without the harmful explosions.

*He who is slow to anger has great understanding,*
*But he who is quick-tempered exalts folly.*
PROVERBS 14:29

THIS VERSE IS not just about our duty to give to the less fortunate. It's also about our *attitude* toward the less fortunate. It's easy to look down on those who lack material resources, social status, or proper manners—even when we are helping them. But it's not the way God wants it. When we treat each other badly, our behavior reflects on the Father!

The real secret to helping the needy, of course, is to realize that we're *all* needy in one way or another. Some of us need food or money or shelter— and some of us are in a position to provide this. Some of us need security or self-confidence or encouragement—and others of us can help. But we all need God's gracious love—and this he gives freely. It's only right for us to do the same.

> *He who oppresses the poor reproaches his Maker,*
> *But he who is gracious to the needy honors Him.*
> PROVERBS 14:31

*The greatest remedy for anger is delay.*
SENECA

*A gentle answer turns away wrath,
But a harsh word stirs up anger.*
PROVERBS 15:1

SOMETIMES ALL IT TAKES to defuse a tense situation is a calm, soft-spoken reply. Avoiding a show of strength in our speech can keep conflict from escalating and keep conversation or negotiation at a level where true meeting of minds is possible. As a bonus, you'll find that low-key, thoughtful speech wins you the respect of others.

Like all wise actions, though, soft answers may take some practice. The most helpful approach may be to just "take ten" whenever you feel yourself growing angry. When you find your mouth opens to let out an angry word, close it, count to ten, and consider whether there's a better way to get your point across.

IF YOU WANT TO improve your appearance, the place to begin is not at the gym or the drugstore—but in your heart! A smile can be faked. A cheerful manner can be pasted over a gloomy spirit. Sooner or later, though, the inner you will show up on the outside. Chronic anxiety reveals itself in a wrinkled brow and a strained expression. Habitual rage shows in clipped speech and clenched fists. And a joyful, peaceful spirit inevitably shines forth in compassionate eyes, a radiant smile, and a confident posture. So ask yourself as you begin your self-improvement program (even before you head out for the gym): *Am I on good terms with the Lord? Am I growing in my faith? Am I seeking help for spiritual or emotional hurts and taking steps to heal my relationships? Am I praying and spending time in the Word?* Take care of the inside—and the outside will eventually take care of itself.

*A joyful heart makes a cheerful face,*
*But when the heart is sad, the spirit is broken.*
PROVERBS 15:13

THE BEST WAY TO get something done right is to bring the Lord in it from the beginning. Share your ideas and your goals with God in prayer. Seek his will about how—and whether!—to tackle the project. Then, as the plans take shape in your head and your heart, you can proceed with them in confidence that the Lord will lend you the strength and intelligence and perseverance you need to get the job done.

*Commit your works to the Lord, And your plans will be established.*
PROVERBS
16:3

45

THERE'S ONLY ONE WAY to handle sin—and that's with God's help!

Only through his persistent love—which led eventually to the sacrifice of his Son—was humanity given a solution to its built-in tendency to ruin everything we touch. Only through his merciful love can we hope to find forgiveness of our stubborn selfishness and willfulness. And only through his power and his truth—can we have the strength to turn from sin when it tempts us.

*When God sends us evil, He sends with it the wherewithal to conquer it.*
PAUL VINCENT CARROLL

*By lovingkindness and truth iniquity is atoned for, And by the fear of the Lord one keeps away from evil.*
PROVERBS 16:6

*God please defend me
from myself.*
SPANISH PROVERB

*It is better to be of
a humble spirit with
the lowly,
Than to divide the spoil
with the proud.*
PROVERBS 16:19

SOME KINDS OF SUCCESS are worse than failure! If you achieve success by stepping on other people—or if you let your good fortune go to your head—you'll be in peril of losing your soul. If you're at one of those points in life when all seems to be going well and you're climbing toward the summit of success, it's crucial that you take time out for a reality check. Remember who you are—a child of God who is being handed a challenge along with the opportunities. Remember who you're not—a uniquely entitled human being whose special gifts allow him to break any rules he sees fit. And remember most of all who God is—the ultimate Judge of who is successful. A little humility can save you from a lot of heartache.

*Where man's method fails and can reach no higher, there God's method begins.*
JAY RUYSBROECK

WE HUMANS HAVE devised all sorts of little gimmicks to help us make decisions. When we're little, it's "eeny, meeny, miny, moe." As we grow older it may be the flip of a coin. For bigger decisions, we may make lists of pros and cons, consult wise advisors, pray fervently…and then do the best we can.

In all of this, the important thing to keep in mind is that God is sovereign over all human affairs—including our decisions large and small. Even what may appears to be chance is really part of God's design. That doesn't exempt us from wise decision making, but it should take a little of the pressure off!

*The lot is cast into the lap,*
*But its every decision is from the Lord.*
PROVERBS 16:33

THERE ARE NO GENERATION GAPS when we honor everybody's position within a family. Children are sources of hope and joy—they literally are the family's future. Parents are sources of sustenance, protection, and care—they are the caretakers of the family's present. Grandparents are sources of stability, wisdom, and memory—they are living treasuries of the family's past. And all family members, of course, are individuals in their own right, each uniquely contributing to the family's common life. When you think about it, it's an outstanding system—something only a good and loving God could have thought of!

*Grandchildren are the crown of old men,*
*And the glory of sons is their fathers.*
PROVERBS 17:6

FRIENDS ARE GREAT TO HAVE—all the time. Families are a real blessing—usually. But it's when life gets rough and bad things happen that the true value of loyal friends and a supportive family becomes clear. When illness or death strike, when unemployment stings, when financial difficulties or personal struggles weigh you down—that's when you need the practical and emotional support of those who know you well and love you anyway.

> *A friend loves at all times,*
> *And a brother is born for adversity.*
> PROVERBS 17:17

Because this is true, it seems only wise to pay attention to building friendships and cultivating warm family relationships. Share lunches. Help with chores. Call just to say hello. Strengthen the bonds of loyalty and affection until they are strong enough to support you all!

50

CONTEMPT, DISHONOR, and reproach are the three children of wickedness. Shameful deeds—sexual transgressions, political manipulations, financial misdeeds—often end in public disgrace. But even if they don't, they still carry consequences: self-contempt, private dishonor, self-reproach…and alienation from God and one's own best self. You avoid a lot of pain by following God's way.

*He that boasts of his own knowledge proclaims his own ignorance.*
GERMAN PROVERB

*When a wicked man comes, contempt also comes,*
*And with dishonor comes reproach.*
PROVERBS 18:3

REMEMBER THERE ARE ALWAYS two sides to every story—at least. First impressions can be misleading, so it is always wise to get as many facts as possible before making a judgment. Nine times out of ten, a delayed decision will be a smarter one.

> *The first to plead his case seems just,*
> *Until another comes and examines him.*
>
> PROVERBS 18:17

*Go often to the house of the friend, for weeds choke the unused path.*

RALPH WALDO EMERSON

WHEN IT COMES TO FRIENDS, quality is definitely more important than quantity. It's better to have one friend you know you can trust than a dozen guys whose only real connection with you is hanging out and having a good time. A real friend is interested in your well-being. He'll stand up for you when you face trouble and won't push you into destructive behavior the way a group of buddies might.

It's not necessarily harmful to have many friends. But it can be harmful to spend time with a lot of "acquaintances" who aren't *really* friends.

*A man of many friends comes to ruin,*
*But there is a friend who sticks closer than a brother.*

PROVERBS 18:24

IT'S A TELLTALE SIGN of foolishness and immaturity to mess up your life and then blame someone else—even God—for your failures. You take a step toward wisdom when you own up to your own shortcomings and take responsibility for them. Once you've done that, you're halfway to solving whatever problem you have encountered.

*The foolishness of man subverts his way,*
*And his heart rages against the Lord.*
PROVERBS 19:3

FOR MOST FATHERS, the issue of disciplining children is not truly one of life and death—at least not on the surface. But if you shirk your responsibility to train your children while they are small, you leave them vulnerable to the dangers that await an undisciplined adult in the world. In some situations, the consequences of unbridled behavior could well be death—either physical or spiritual. But even the "lesser evils" that arise from a lack of discipline—such as failed plans, broken relationships, and inability to reach potential—are painful enough. Loving your children means caring enough to give them the physical and emotional tools they will need to live in the world—including self-discipline.

*Discipline your son while there is hope,*
*And do not desire his death.*
PROVERBS 19:18

*The sluggard does not plow after the autumn,*
*So he begs during the harvest and has nothing.*

PROVERBS 20:4

YOU CAN'T REST on your laurels after a task is completed, even if it has been a success. Instead, you need to be thinking and preparing for what you will do next. As long as we are on this earth, we all have work to do—and for most of us, that work is what enables us and our families to live. So take a short rest if you need it, then grab your "plow" and don't procrastinate. It's time to start preparing for the next season of harvest.

56

*Live so that the preacher can tell the truth at your funeral.*
AUTHOR UNKNOWN

EVERY DAY, AS YOU LIVE, you are writing a story that will shape your children's lives. Not only are they learning from you now; they will continue to learn as they look back and remember what kind of man you are. The greatest legacy you can leave them is a Christian heritage and the knowledge that they lived with a man of honor—someone who kept his promises, defended the weak, and obeyed God.

*A righteous man who walks in his integrity—*
*How blessed are his sons after him.*
PROVERBS 20:7

Hᴏᴡ ᴍᴀɴʏ ᴏʟᴅᴇʀ ᴘᴇᴏᴘʟᴇ have complained that "youth is wasted on the young"—that they wish the wisdom and experience of age could be combined with a young person's energy and drive. But God made us this way on purpose. Every age has its advantage and disadvantage—especially if we help one another.

The advantage of youth is strength, high energy, resilience, and the willingness

> *The glory of young men is their strength,*
> *And the honor of old men is their gray hair.*
> Pʀᴏᴠᴇʀʙs 20:29

to try something new. Most young people relish challenges—the tougher and harder the better. But young people often lack the confidence and balance that comes with experience. They may not know it, but deep inside they crave limits and direction. Young people were built for God, and without God as the center of their lives they become frustrated and confused, desperately grasping for and searching for security.

"YOU'LL GET WHAT YOU DESERVE." That's a phrase that means different things to different people. Someone who has worked diligently and done the right thing might expect a reward—praise, recognition, or money. Someone who has cut corners and broken rules would rightly fear punishment or shame. Something deep within us desires that kind of justice. It's part of being created in our just Father's image.

At the same time, we need to remember that we are *all* sinners—and if we get what we really deserve, we're in big trouble. We can only thank our God that his justice is balanced with his infinite mercy—that he desires our salvation, not our punishment. God's justice *will* prevail, but because of Jesus we have a chance of *not* getting what we deserve.

*The execution of justice is joy for the righteous,*
*But is terror to the workers of iniquity.*
PROVERBS 21:15

*Train up a child in the way he should go,*
*Even when he is old he will not depart from it.*

PROVERBS 22:6

AS PARENTS WE ARE to use our words, our example, and our authority to teach our children the values we feel are important and the skills and habits that will make them better people. For better or for worse, what they learn in the home is what they will carry into adult life. So train up a child in the way he should go… and walk there yourself as much as you can!

REMEMBER THE FIRST TIME you realized just how fast money can fly away? You may think you have a lot, but it's amazing how quickly it vanishes. Material wealth is part of the material world, which means it just can't last. We can use it as a tool for good—investing it for the future, contributing to God's work, supporting physical needs while focusing on spiritual realities—and continue to taste God's abundance. Or we can misuse it—hoarding it for our own selfish purposes, wielding it to get our own way, or squandering it on foolish pursuits—and end up with empty bank accounts, empty spirits, or both!

*And my inmost being will rejoice,*
*When your lips speak what is right.*

PROVERBS 23:16

STANDING UP FOR TRUTH means more than just being honest ourselves. We are also to support and encourage others who take the risk of speaking the truth. We are to applaud and praise all who have the courage to stand up and be counted for what is right—and try to persuade others to stand up for truth as well.

*Praise makes good men better and bad men worse.*
THOMAS FULLER

THE WORLD IS FULL of beautiful things for us to enjoy—but it's possible for something beautiful to be a person's downfall. It could be a prestigious home, a sleek car, a gorgeous woman, even a delectable meal. Usually it's not evil in itself—though certain pleasurable pursuits have a history of causing trouble!—but it exposes an emotional or spiritual weakness that causes us to want too much of it. If you discover a particular weakness for any of the beautiful things in life—an inability to enjoy them in moderation and keep them in their place—it's better to put yourself in a situation where you won't be tempted. And don't rely on your own judgment in this; the possibility of denial is too great. Ask several wise friends whose advice you trust whether any of the "beautiful things" in your life have become a problem for you—and follow their advice.

*Do not look on the wine when it is red,*
*When it sparkles in the cup,*
*When it goes down smoothly.*

PROVERBS 23:31

*By wisdom a house is built,*
*And by understanding it is established,*
*And by knowledge the rooms are filled*
*With all precious and pleasant riches.*
PROVERBS 24:3

IT TAKES WISDOM, understanding, and knowledge—not to mention creativity and hard work—to locate a house, buy or rent it, and then transform it into a physical environment that nourishes the spirit as well as providing a place to eat and sleep. It takes wisdom, understanding, and knowledge—along with patience, love, and a lot of prayer—to build a family that helps one another, supports one another, solves problems mutually, and lives within a comforting framework of common values. A home that is built with these quality "tools"—the tools of good character—is a treasure-house indeed.

IN THIS ERA of disrespect for government and public office, the words of this proverb are important to remember. We are to respect and honor those who are in authority over us—parents, bosses, police officers, and public office holders. Even if we have difficulty with the personality or politics of the person in question, we can still show respect for the office by speaking civilly, obeying the rules, and praying for the person in question. This doesn't mean we should never voice our opinions or stand up for our beliefs.

*My son, fear the Lord and the King,
Do not associate with those who are given to change.*
PROVERBS 24:21

And eventually, we will have the opportunity to leave home, change jobs, protest a traffic ticket, or vote a politician out of office. But we must always remember that those who are in authority over us are placed there by God. To rebel openly is to rebel against God…and show how little we trust his ability to work through the most unlikely of servants.

A MAN HAS CERTAIN preparations to make before he marries and has a family. He needs a dependable source of income, for instance, and an understanding of basic household finance. He needs enough education to be able to do his work—and enough opportunity to retrain for future work. He needs to know how to work as a partner, to negotiate and communicate. But most of all, he needs an understanding of what God expects from a husband and a father—not macho posturing, but sacrificial, self-giving love. If you're not ready to be God's kind of man, then you're not ready to be a married man. Slow down. Satan rushes in, but the Holy Spirit takes its time.

*Prepare your work outside,*
*And make it ready for*
*yourself in the field;*
*Afterwards, then, build*
*your house.*
PROVERBS 24:27

IT'S EASY TO HAVE too much of a good thing. In fact, trying to get too much of a good thing is a basic aspect of human nature. We tend to want more, more, more, even when more is not good for us. And this is true of food, drink, sex, exercise, sports, any pleasant occupation. It's so easy to cross over the line from "this is great" to groans of "I can't believe I did that!"

The good life is one of moderation, not overindulgence. And moderation can only be achieved with an ongoing attitude of trust and gratitude. We must remember that God is the one who supplies the blessings in the first place and that we can trust him to give us what we need. We don't need to overindulge because we can count on God to give us more, more, more when we need it.

*Have you found honey?*
*Eat only what you need,*
*Lest you have it in*
*excess and vomit it.*
PROVERBS 25:16

HERE'S ONE OF those words of wisdom that really goes against the grain. When we hear that someone we really dislike is in need, we should do what we can to help him. We should respond kindly toward those who have treated us badly or opposed us. There are echoes of this proverb in Jesus' command to love our enemies. And the spiritual and psychological logic behind this hard-to-follow advice is sound. When we respond to bad treatment with good treatment, we make it clear who the bad guy really is! Perhaps we'll embarrass the other person into acting better. But even if that doesn't happen, we'll have God's blessing...along with the satisfaction that we haven't let the ill treatment turn us into somebody we don't want to be.

*If your enemy is hungry, give him food to eat;*
*And if he is thirsty, give him water to drink;*
*For you will heap burning coals on his head,*
*And the Lord will reward you.*

PROVERBS 25:21-22

WHY WOULD A MAN spend a lifetime cultivating righteousness and then suddenly fall off the deep end? We've all heard stories of upstanding citizens who have had affairs, walked out on their families, quit their jobs, developed substance-abuse problems, or simply turned away from God. When a good person falls into such bad behavior, he doesn't just hurt himself; he also disillusions and disappoints those who have learned to rely upon him.

The truth is that we're never "home free" when it comes to sin and self-deception—no matter how many years of righteousness we've put in. That's why we need God's dependable "righteousness maintenance" routine: coming to God regularly with our confessions and our needs, repenting of our sins and accepting forgiveness, reconciling our relationships when something goes wrong, and seeking out wise counselors to support us and hold us accountable.

*Character is much more easily kept than recovered.*
AUTHOR
UNKNOWN

*Like a trampled spring and a polluted well Is a righteous man who gives way before the wicked.*
PROVERBS
25:26

> *A lying tongue hates*
> *those it crushes,*
> *And a flattering*
> *mouth works ruin.*
>
> PROVERBS 26:28

A LIE—even one of the "little white" variety—can be more harmful than it appears because it is a form of manipulation, an attempt to control another person's actions by controlling his access to the facts. At best, lies and flattery (a form of lying) result in shallow relationships, frequent misunderstandings, and a general atmosphere of cynicism and mistrust. At worst—usually when the truth finally emerges—they can flatten another person's ego and destroy his life.

It's been said that "the truth hurts." But truth never hurt quite so deeply and destructively as lies and deception.

SHOULD YOU SPEAK UP when a friend is doing something dangerous and self-destructive? If you care about him, you will— even if the confrontation is difficult. He may listen, or he may respond with anger, but it's still better to say something than to stand by while a friend hurts himself or others.

*Better is open rebuke*
*Than love that is concealed.*
PROVERBS 27:5

71

*Blessed is the influence of one true, loving soul on another.*
GEORGE ELIOT

*Iron sharpens iron,*
*So one man sharpens another.*
PROVERBS 27:17

IT'S TIME TO PUT the myth of the Lone Ranger to rest once and for all. The romantic notion of the man who walks alone and doesn't need anyone except perhaps his horse is simply that—a romantic notion. The truth is that we men need each other for support and encouragement. We need men who will model righteous living for us, who will hold us accountable for how we live, and who will provide practical support during the difficult periods of our lives. We also need the opportunity to provide those things for other men. When we meet these needs for each other, we can all be stronger, better people.

HOW A MAN RESPONDS to a compliment and praise is a test of his character. Some people react gruffly—as if the person giving the praise were delivering an inappropriate and unwanted gift. Others receive the compliment haughtily, like a required tribute. Still others can't receive praise without immediately returning it—so that an exchange of pleasantries becomes a game of one-upmanship.

What is the better alternative—the response that shows the healthiest character? The most effective way to answer to a compliment is with gratitude and humility—with a simple and heartfelt "thank you."

*The crucible is for silver and the furnace for gold, And a man is tested by the praise accorded him.*
PROVERBS 27:21

*He who conceals his transgressions will not prosper,*
*But he who confesses and forsakes them will find compassion.*

PROVERBS 28:13

THERE IS SOMETHING about unconfessed sin that hardens the heart. The longer we go without getting right with God, the more set we become in our ways, and the more reluctant we are to come to him at all. It's like not going to the doctor because you're embarrassed that you haven't gone in such a long time—and because you're afraid of what the doctor might find! The regular process of coming clean to God and receiving his forgiveness is important to growing as a healthy human being. But even if it's been a long time since your last "check up," it's worth coming in. The Great Physician can take care of whatever needs fixing—even a crusty, reluctant heart.

Don't be in too much of a hurry to make your financial mark on the world. The get-rich-quick mindset is a trap that draws people into foolish decisions. They embark on risky ventures without checking out the possible consequences, they become easy prey for con artists, or they may be tempted to cut their own ethical corners. Don't risk material and moral bankruptcy—slow and steady is a far better strategy for both earning and investing. Set your goals, make your plan, and stick to your plan.

*A faithful man will abound*
*with blessings,*
*But he who makes haste to*
*be rich will not go unpunished.*
PROVERBS 28:20

HOW DO YOU FEEL when you wake up in the morning? Tired and depressed, wondering what bad things will happen that day, and waiting for the other shoe to drop? Or cheerful and enthusiastic, ready for whatever blessings life will hand you that day? Keeping your conscience clean is one way to ensure that you wake up with a song on your lips. There's nothing like guilt and fear and the simple weight of not being right with God to put a damper on your day. That's why it's so helpful to come to God on a daily basis, confessing your sins and accepting God's forgiveness, sharing your problems and giving them to God. Keeping up to date with the Lord won't guarantee you'll sing in the shower—he didn't make us all morning people!—but it will lighten your heart and help you move more joyfully through your day.

*When we cannot find contentment in ourselves, it is useless to seek it elsewhere.*
FRANÇOIS, DUC DE LA ROCHEFOUCAULD

*By transgression an evil man is ensnared, But the righteous sings and rejoices.*
PROVERBS 29:6

*Aim at heaven and you will get earth thrown in. Aim at earth and you will get neither.*
C. S. LEWIS

*Where there is no vision, the people are unrestrained, But happy is he who keeps the law.*
PROVERBS 29:18

I T'S A FACT OF LIFE that your future won't go exactly as you planned. But it's also a fact of life that if you *don't* plan, your future isn't likely to go anywhere. If you have no goals, no vision, you'll probably be tossed to and fro by things that happen to you and by your own appetites. Without a sense of purpose, it's hard to know what to do next. That's why you need the big picture that the process of goal setting and planning offers you. You also need the stability that comes from following God's plan as outlined in his Word. God has the big picture on the universe and his plans will always—in his timing—work out. And that's the ultimate fact of life.

*An excellent wife, who can find?*
*For her worth is far above jewels.*

PROVERBS 31:10

CHOOSING A WIFE is one of the most important decisions a man will ever make. But some men seem to put more energy and thought into buying a car than they do into choosing a life's partner. If they like her, if they get along well with her, if there is good sexual chemistry, and if they're ready to settle down…that more or less decides it.

But so much is at stake in a marriage! It's a decision you'll live with every day of your life. A good partnership will make every other aspect of life go more smoothly. A mismatch can send both of you limping through life, dragging along a nonsupportive partner—or shredded by a painful divorce. It just makes sense to choose a marriage partner with thoughtfulness and a lot of prayer.

THE BOTTOM LINE for choosing a wife, of course, should be her spiritual commitment. An honorable woman who fears the Lord and makes it a priority to grow in him has a huge advantage when it comes to being a good life partner. She won't be perfect—no person is. She may struggle with emotional difficulties and relational hang-ups—so may you. She may or may not be beautiful in a conventional way—though it's good if there is some sort of "spark" between you. But if she is a woman of prayer, a woman who understands human sinfulness and God's forgiveness, and a woman who is willing to obey God's Word—you'll both come out ahead in your life together. That's especially true if you make prayer, forgiveness, and obedience a priority as well!

> *Charm is deceitful and beauty is vain,*
> *But a woman who fears the Lord, she shall be praised.*
> PROVERBS 31:30

# A Closing Word

*Conduct is what we do; character is what we are. Conduct is the outward life; character is the life unseen, hidden within, yet evidenced by that which is seen. Conduct is external, seen from without; character is internal—operating within. . .character is the state of the heart, conduct is its outward expression. Character is the root of the tree, conduct, the fruit it bears.*

E.M. BOUNDS

*A wise man will hear and increase in learning,*
*And a man of understanding will acquire wise counsel,*
*To understand a proverb and a figure,*
*The words of the wise and their riddles.*

PROVERBS 1:5-6